AF270212

# Chihuahuas

by Grace Hansen

DOGS

Abdo Kids

Abdo Kids Jumbo is an Imprint of Abdo Kids
abdobooks.com

**abdobooks.com**

Published by Abdo Kids, a division of ABDO, P.O. Box 398166, Minneapolis, Minnesota 55439.
Copyright © 2022 by Abdo Consulting Group, Inc. International copyrights reserved in all countries.
No part of this book may be reproduced in any form without written permission from the publisher.
Abdo Kids Jumbo™ is a trademark and logo of Abdo Kids.

Printed in China

052021

092021

THIS BOOK CONTAINS
RECYCLED MATERIALS

Photo Credits: iStock, Shutterstock, Thinkstock

Production Contributors: Teddy Borth, Jennie Forsberg, Grace Hansen
Design Contributors: Dorothy Toth, Pakou Moua

Library of Congress Control Number: 2020947652
Publisher's Cataloging-in-Publication Data

Names: Hansen, Grace, author.
Title: Chihuahuas / by Grace Hansen
Description: Minneapolis, Minnesota : Abdo Kids, 2022 | Series: Dogs | Includes online resources and
    index.
Identifiers: ISBN 9781098206000 (lib. bdg.) | ISBN 9781098206567 (ebook) | ISBN 9781098206840
    (Read-to-Me ebook)
Subjects: LCSH: Chihuahua (Dog breed)--Juvenile literature. | Toy dogs--Juvenile literature. | Dogs--
    Juvenile literature. | Animal behavior--Juvenile literature.
Classification: DDC 599.772--dc23

# Table of Contents

## Chihuahuas

Chihuahuas are a very old dog breed. They were named in the mid-1800s after Chihuahua, Mexico. However, they have been popular pets for hundreds of years.

United States
Mexico
Chihuahua
N
W
E
S

Chihuahuas are the smallest dog breed. They weigh less than 6 pounds (3 kg). They are just 6 to 9 inches (15-23 cm) tall.

A Chihuahua's head is small and round. Its ears are large and stand up on its head. The dog's eyes are full, round, and set far apart.

Chihuahuas can have long or short coats. The coats can be many colors including **fawn**, red, black, and white. They can also have markings.

## Grooming

Chihuahuas with long coats should be brushed weekly. All Chihuahuas should be bathed around once a month.

13

## Exercise

Chihuahuas prefer shorter walks. But they can handle longer walks at a slower pace.

## Personality

Though tiny in size, Chihuahuas have big personalities. They are also very smart and **sensitive**. They respond well to gentle training.

Chihuahuas are very attached to their owners. They like to go wherever their owners go.

Chihuahuas are tough pups. But they are physically small and **fragile**. Their families should always handle them with care.

# More Facts

- Dogs resembling Chihuahuas can be found in **ancient** paintings in Mexico.

- The El Paso Chihuahuas are a minor league baseball team located in El Paso, Texas. Their mascot is Chico, a tough Chihuahua!

- *Beverly Hills Chihuahua* is a 2008 comedy film that follows the adventures of Chihuahuas Chloe and Papi.

# Glossary

**ancient** – very old.

**breed** – a particular type of animal.

**fawn** – yellowish tan.

**fragile** – easily hurt.

**sensitive** – highly aware or feeling things strongly.

# Index

Visit **abdokids.com** to access crafts, games, videos, and more!